ESSENTIAL 101 TIPS

GOLF

ESSENTIAL TIPS
101

GOLF

Peter Ballingall

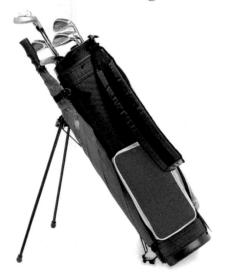

A DORLING KINDERSLEY BOOK

Editor James Harrison
Art Editor Clive Hayball
DTP Designer Mark Bracey
Series Editor Charlotte Davies
Managing Art Editor Amanda Lunn
Production Controller Louise Daly
US Editor Laaren Brown

PUBLISHER'S NOTE
The instructions in this book are assumed for right-handed golfers,
and where appropriate should be reversed for left-handed golfers.

First published in Canada in 1995 by
Fenn Publishing Company Ltd.
34 Nixon Road, Bolton, Ontario, L7E 1W2, Canada
Reprinted 1996

ISBN 1-55168-035-1

Text film output by The Right Type, Great Britain
Reproduced by Colourscan, Singapore
Printed and bound by Graphicom, Italy

ESSENTIAL TIPS

ADDRESSING
THE BALL

SWING
WITH SUCCESS

CLOTHING & EQUIPMENT

1 A SURE FOOTING

Think about this: when you play golf you are likely to walk about 4 miles (6 km) up and down hills on fairly rough, often wet and muddy, terrain. Spiked shoes are a must because they provide a nonslip base when you are swinging on spongy ground. They also secure a firmer foothold than pebble-soled or ribbed shoes – especially vital on slopes – and so aid the proper body weight transfer needed in the swing.

Golf shoes for summer play should still have spikes

All-purpose spiked shoe for best swing support

2 GLOVES FOR GRIP

A glove should fit like a second skin. Its purpose is to improve adhesion between your hand and the handle of the club. Choose thin leather gloves. They give the best feel. Before buying, check that the gloves are resistant to shrinkage from perspiration and rain showers. They may be hand-washable. Once the leather stretches and the glove becomes loose, you must replace it.

THIN LEATHER GLOVES

3 GOLF MITTENS

Warm hands are essential in cold playing conditions. If your hands are cold you will not achieve a decent grip. Professionals always wear mittens between shots when cold or wet weather conditions dictate. In such weather, when not playing a shot, wear nylon fiber mittens to keep your hands warm and dry.

INSULATED MITTENS FOR WARM HANDS

4 RAINWEAR

Always be prepared for wet weather. Carry a lightweight waterproof jacket and pull-on pants in your bag. Make sure that the fit allows you to make a full, unencumbered swing. Choose lightweight synthetic fabrics that stop water from seeping in while letting perspiration out.

Lightweight jacket

WET CARE △
Always drip-dry your rain gear after each game. It will last much longer.

◁ DRY FEET
In extremely wet conditions these spiked golf boots are ideal.

IF LIGHTNING STRIKES
If you are caught in a thunderstorm, do not seek shelter under trees. Instead, head for a bunker. Avoid using a steel-shafted umbrella as it could conduct lightning.

5 CORRECT CLOTHES

Comfort is a must when choosing golf clothing. Always make sure your golf clothes allow you ample room to swing properly without constrictions. Clothes must also be neat since most clubs will not permit jeans, collarless shirts, cut-offs, or tank tops.

Short-sleeved shirt for warm weather

◁ △ SHIRTS
Golf or sports shirts with sleeves and collars are essential items.

Light, cool cotton for hot summer play

TROUSERS ▷
Sensible slacks are the order of the day. They allow freedom of twisting as you swing.

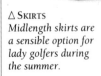

△ SKIRTS
Midlength skirts are a sensible option for lady golfers during the summer.

SWEATERS ▷
Short-sleeved sweaters prevent chills; bear in mind that you could be playing for well over four hours.

△ HATS
For play in the sun wear a visor. For wet play choose waterproof hats.

△ WINDBREAKERS
Windbreakers cut out the windchill factor, even in summer.

SOCKS ▷
Wear insulated socks in winter, and cushioned socks with shorts.

6 UMBRELLA CHOICE

Umbrellas offer good protection when you are just standing around, but they can be disruptive to your rhythm and tempo when preparing to play a shot. Fiberglass models are safest if you are caught out in a lightning storm.

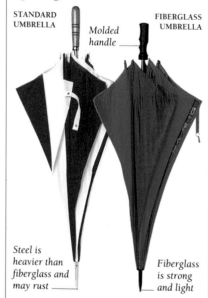

STANDARD UMBRELLA

Molded handle

FIBERGLASS UMBRELLA

Steel is heavier than fiberglass and may rust

Fiberglass is strong and light

7 WET WEATHER CARE

- Take several playing gloves in case one gets soaking wet.
- Hook a towel inside the umbrella where it will stay dry. Use it to wipe off the moisture from the grips.
- Use the hood of the bag to keep your clubs dry when not in play.

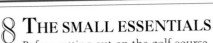

8 THE SMALL ESSENTIALS

Before setting out on the golf course, check that in your bag or pocket you have a sufficient number of the small essentials that will guarantee a smoother round: tees, ball mark repairer, coin or ball marker, pencil, small towel, and wet sponge. A spare pair of shoelaces may come in handy too.

plastic tee

wooden tee

◁△ **TEES**
Pros prefer wooden tees although they break. Plastic tees are stronger.

◁ **MARKERS**
Use specially made markers, or small coins, to mark your ball on the green if it is in the way of your partner's ball.

◁ **GRASS REPAIRERS**
Useful for repairing indent marks on the green and to clean dirt from club face grooves.

TOWEL ▷
On a wet day this is handy for wiping the club face and grip dry before each shot.

△ **SPONGER**
This is useful for cleaning out dirt from the golf ball's dimples after each hole.

◁ **PENCIL / PEN**
Have these at hand to write down your, and your partner's, score.

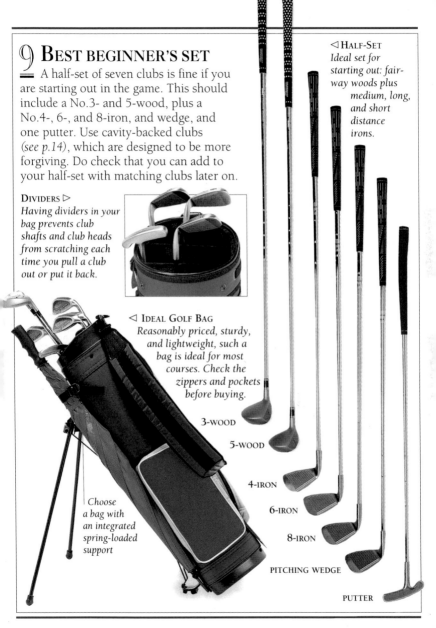

9 BEST BEGINNER'S SET

A half-set of seven clubs is fine if you are starting out in the game. This should include a No.3- and 5-wood, plus a No.4-, 6-, and 8-iron, and wedge, and one putter. Use cavity-backed clubs (*see p.14*), which are designed to be more forgiving. Do check that you can add to your half-set with matching clubs later on.

(see p.14)

△ **HALF-SET**
Ideal set for starting out: fairway woods plus medium, long, and short distance irons.

DIVIDERS ▷
Having dividers in your bag prevents club shafts and club heads from scratching each time you pull a club out or put it back.

△ **IDEAL GOLF BAG**
Reasonably priced, sturdy, and lightweight, such a bag is ideal for most courses. Check the zippers and pockets before buying.

3-WOOD

5-WOOD

Choose a bag with an integrated spring-loaded support

4-IRON

6-IRON

8-IRON

PITCHING WEDGE

PUTTER

10 CAST OR FORGED IRONS?

If you are a beginner, choose cast irons. These are based on a design called "peripheral weighting," where the mass of the club head is located at the outside edges. This allows a larger sweet spot area on the club face which minimizes the effects of poor shots. Novices need this "forgiveness," but good players prefer the feel of forged irons.

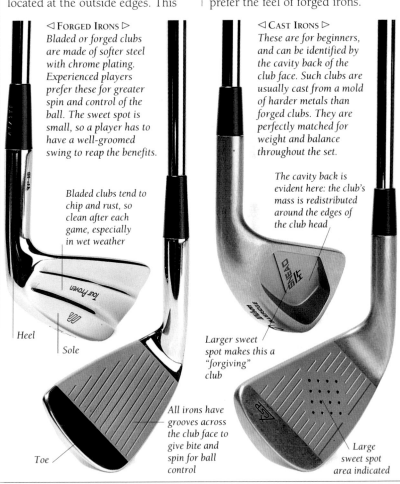

◁ FORGED IRONS ▷
Bladed or forged clubs are made of softer steel with chrome plating. Experienced players prefer these for greater spin and control of the ball. The sweet spot is small, so a player has to have a well-groomed swing to reap the benefits.

Bladed clubs tend to chip and rust, so clean after each game, especially in wet weather

Heel

Sole

Toe

◁ CAST IRONS ▷
These are for beginners, and can be identified by the cavity back of the club face. Such clubs are usually cast from a mold of harder metals than forged clubs. They are perfectly matched for weight and balance throughout the set.

The cavity back is evident here: the club's mass is redistributed around the edges of the club head

Larger sweet spot makes this a "forgiving" club

All irons have grooves across the club face to give bite and spin for ball control

Large sweet spot area indicated

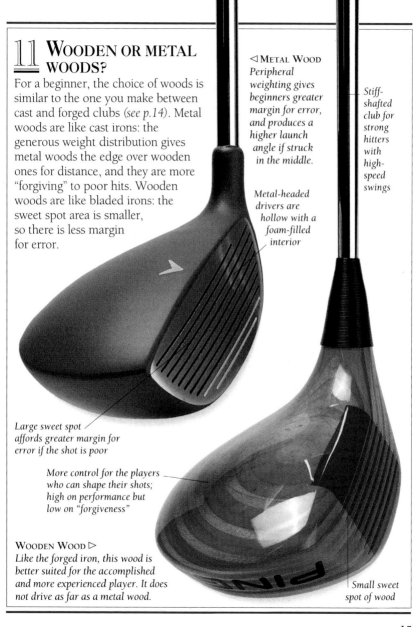

11 WOODEN OR METAL WOODS?

For a beginner, the choice of woods is similar to the one you make between cast and forged clubs (see p.14). Metal woods are like cast irons: the generous weight distribution gives metal woods the edge over wooden ones for distance, and they are more "forgiving" to poor hits. Wooden woods are like bladed irons: the sweet spot area is smaller, so there is less margin for error.

◁ METAL WOOD
Peripheral weighting gives beginners greater margin for error, and produces a higher launch angle if struck in the middle.

Stiff-shafted club for strong hitters with high-speed swings

Metal-headed drivers are hollow with a foam-filled interior

Large sweet spot affords greater margin for error if the shot is poor

More control for the players who can shape their shots; high on performance but low on "forgiveness"

WOODEN WOOD ▷
Like the forged iron, this wood is better suited for the accomplished and more experienced player. It does not drive as far as a metal wood.

Small sweet spot of wood

12 WHICH SHAFT FLEX?

When choosing a club, ask about the shaft flex; that is, how much it bends. There are five types:

- "Extra stiff" is for professionals.
- "Stiff" is for low-handicap golfers and younger players.
- "Medium" is for the average club golfer of all levels.
- "Whippy" is for older golfers as well as for taller ladies.
- "Ladies' flex," as its name suggests, is for lady golfers. Waggle a club in front of you: can you feel the weight of the club head responding? If so, that flex should suit you.

Most widely used shaft in every price range, with flexes to suit every player

Produces extra flex, with little torque, for more distance and control

Take care with graphite shafts as the outer coating can wear through from constant rubbing against the rim of the golf bag

STEEL SHAFT

BORON-REINFORCED SHAFT

COLORED GRAPHITE SHAFT

13 CHECK THAT THE CLUBS FIT

The loft and lie on a set of clubs do not vary from one manufacturer to the next, but can be altered to suit the height and playing strength of the golfer.

A tall player requires a longer shaft, but a shorter player should never play with shorter shafts. The lie can be adjusted to guarantee that the clubs sit perfectly. Try this coin test.

LIE TOO UPRIGHT
Take up the address position: if the coin won't slip under the club toe, the lie of the club is too upright.

LIE TOO FLAT
If the coin slips easily under the club toe to halfway along, the lie is too flat, and this needs to be adjusted.

CORRECT ANGLE OF LIE
If the coin slips just under the front of club toe, then the club is at the correct angle for your height.

14 PUTTER PREFERENCES

There are five main types of putter: the traditional blade, heel-toe weighted, center-shafted, mallet-headed, and "wacky." Take one that suits you for length and lie. These putters vary in length from 34–37 in (86–94 cm) but broomhandle clubs are much taller. Putters often have a visible sweet spot line or dot to guide your stroke. Use it as a guide.

◁ VARIATIONS ▷
Ladies' putters are lighter and shorter. Youngsters can start with these.

Classic center-shafted putter design

Sweet spot

Toe

Heel

△ TRY BEFORE YOU BUY
Ask if you can try out a putter before you buy. A pro should be happy to tape up the face and let you test it on the practice green.

INLAID LINES SHOW SWEET SPOT AREA

15 SWEET SPOT MARKER

The sweet spot is the area where the mass of the club, or density, is concentrated. Although it is often marked on the putter, you can also find it by holding the club lightly between forefinger and thumb and letting the club hang freely. Now tap along the blade with your other forefinger until the putter rebounds without twisting. That's the sweet spot.

17

16 WHICH BALL?

Golf ball selection can be as critical as choosing the right clubs. Size is governed by the rules, so it's the differences in aerodynamic properties — the lift, drag, and spin — and the "feel" that you will have to choose among.

Solid, more durable resin core

Number is purely for identification

2
DUNLOP
Powermax

Wound construction for durability

Surlyn cover is almost indestructible and best for beginners

Solid center

TWO-PIECE BALL △
Best suited for the less experienced player, this ball is extremely strong and designed to create topspin as well as distance. It is not as controllable around the green as the ball tends to bounce off the club face.

1
Maxfli
DDH 500

THREE-PIECE △
SURLYN BALL
This is ideal for the amateur golfer seeking both distance and durability. Not as easily controlled around the green as the softer-covered balata ball.

Wound yarn

Liquid center for superb feel

Liquid-filled membrane barrier to wound section

THREE-PIECE BALATA COVER ▷
This is the ball that is used by low-handicap amateurs as well as professionals. Although it gives a good feel, responds to spin, and putts well, it is very expensive and is easily damaged – barely surviving one round of golf.

Soft, synthetic balata cover for spin control

Titleist
1

17 MARKING A BALL

Before you play, mark your golf balls with a ballpoint pen, or similar marker, to identify them at a glance (even though golf balls are stamped for identification purposes). You will incur a penalty if you play or pick up a wrong ball.

MARK A DIMPLE OR TWO WITH A PEN

18 KEEPING GRIPS CLEAN

The ridges and grooves on the grip provide you with friction for a secure hold against your hand. Always scrub them after a game to remove grease and dirt. If worn down, have the handles regripped.

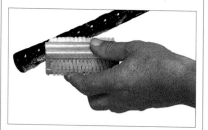

SCRUB WITH HARD BRUSH TO CLEAN GRIPS

19 KEEPING GROOVES CLEAN

Try to keep the grooves in the club face free from dirt and grit at all times. It's not difficult to do and it is amazing how looking down at a dirty club face can breed a lack of confidence. More importantly, it can affect performance as the grooves are designed to generate backspin.

1 After a game, wipe the grooves with a brush and dishwashing liquid under warm running water.

2 Towel dry to remove any leftover water from the club face, which could cause rusting later .

3 Keep some spare tees handy to remove dirt or debris in the grooves while out on the course.

20 HOW TO BUY USED CLUBS

Almost every golf professional's shop has used clubs for sale – often complete with a secondhand bag. There's nothing wrong with buying used clubs, especially if you are starting out in golf, but do check that the club heads and shafts have no rust and ask the professional if you can hit some balls on the practice tee to see if the set suits you.

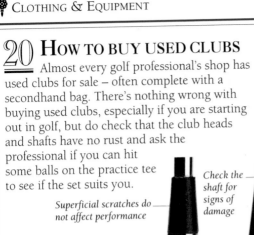

Superficial scratches do not affect performance

Check the shaft for signs of damage

Look for cracks in the neck

IRONS ▷
Iron heads are almost indestructible, but check that the grooves are not so worn down as to be indistinct. Don't be put off by minor surface scratches as these will not affect club-to-ball impact.

Avoid clubs with worn-down grooves and rust

Blemishes are unsightly but not critical

GRIPS △
Check if the grips feel "tacky" or rough, not smooth. You can ask the club shop to regrip these.

WOODS ▷
Look for damage like cracks in the neck and wear and tear on the club face and sole. Metal woods are generally less prone to damage .

△ THE SOLE
Damage to the sole plate is an obvious sign of how the previous owner has treated the wood. Avoid this club.

If the insert is damaged, but you like the club's feel, a club pro could restore it for you

21 SELECTING A BAG

New bags are not too expensive and are well worth the investment. Ultimately, consider having two: one lightweight bag for carrying when winter rules may prohibit carts, as well as for taking on planes; and one larger and strengthened bag that is designed to take a full set of 14 clubs and to be carried on a cart.

◁▽ BAGS
Look for sturdy straps, strong zippers, and ample pockets.

Head covers protect clubs against scuffing

LIGHTWEIGHT

Look for an easy-folding cart

Quick lock-on adjusters

STRENGTHENED

Good pockets for carrying wet-weather gear

△▷ CARTS
Choose a sturdy cart with quick-release straps and wide wheels for good stability.

Towel for cleaning and drying clubs and balls

UNDERSTANDING BASIC GRIPS

22 THE OVERLAPPING GRIP

There are several grips to choose from, but the overlapping grip, also called the Vardon grip, is the most widely used and the best for most golfers, except those with small hands, *(see pp.24–27 for alternative grips and variations)*. Golf is 98 percent setup and 2 percent start, and setup revolves around your grip. Establishing a "grip-it-right" routine is vital for control of the club face and of the ball.

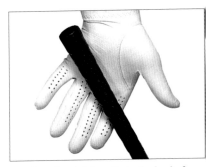

1 Place the club handle in the heel of the left hand and across the palm so that it rests diagonally from the heel to the middle of the left forefinger.

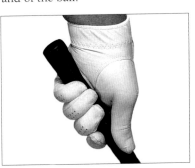

2 As you close your hand, the club should sit in the crook of the forefinger. Wrap the fingers around for a light – not tight – and secure grip.

3 The thumb should now sit just to the right of center on top of the handle. The V formed by the forefinger and thumb should point up to your right ear.

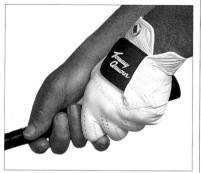

4 Position the right hand so that the handle of the club rests in the crook of the middle two fingers – not in the base of the two fingers.

5 Overlap the knuckle of the forefinger of the left hand with the little finger of the right hand. Thumb and forefinger should have an easy hold on the handle.

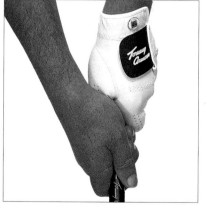

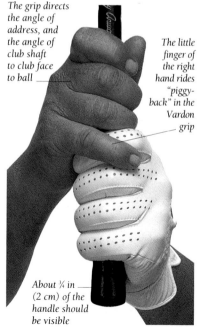

The grip directs the angle of address, and the angle of club shaft to club face to ball

The little finger of the right hand rides "piggy-back" in the Vardon grip

6 Rest your right thumb on the front face of the grip and to the left of the club shaft, so that it now forms a triggerlike position with your right forefinger.

7 Make sure to check that the V created where your right thumb and forefinger have met over the handle now points up to the right shoulder.

About ¾ in (2 cm) of the handle should be visible

23 INTERLOCKING METHOD

If you have a weak grip, or small hands, try the interlocking grip. This grip is widely used by amateurs, though seldom employed by professionals. As its name suggests, the key difference here is that the little finger and forefinger of opposite hands are interlocked.

1 Rest the handle in the palm of your left hand, diagonally across the palm. Keep the forefinger pointing down.

2 Bring the right hand under the left, slotting in the last two fingers of the right hand between the left-hand forefinger.

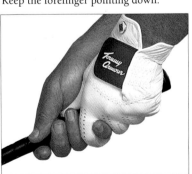

3 Rest the club in the crook of the two middle fingers of the right hand. Close the right hand snugly over the left.

4 The left thumb should be encased in the right hand and your fingers should feel firm but not rigid.

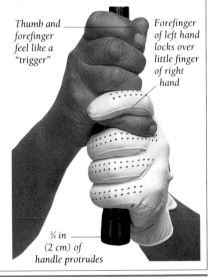

Thumb and forefinger feel like a "trigger"

Forefinger of left hand locks over little finger of right hand

¾ in (2 cm) of handle protrudes

24 TWO-HANDED (BASEBALL) METHOD

With this grip, all eight fingers of both hands are on the handle. Both palms face each other but do not overlap. Adults with small hands, and youngsters, can benefit from this variation. The forefinger and little finger of opposite hands rest side-by-side.

1 Make a pistol-like grip with the fingers around the handle close to the butt. The thumb lies just to the right.

2 Bring the right hand toward the grip and try to keep both palms facing each other. Right-hand pad encases left thumb.

3 All four fingers of your right hand should now wrap around the handle lightly but firmly with the thumb on top.

4 The little finger of the right hand lies comfortably beside, but not over, the forefinger of the left hand.

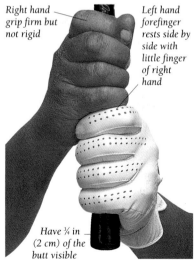

Right hand grip firm but not rigid

Left hand forefinger rests side by side with little finger of right hand

Have ¼ in (2 cm) of the butt visible

25 GRIP TEST

Whichever grip you adopt, the hold must be light not tight. A light grip enables you to make a free, uninhibited swing, to achieve club head speed and therefore distance. To get used to the correct left-hand grip, suspend the club from the heel of the left hand as shown and into the left forefinger. You will feel the weight of the club head, yet the club is securely placed. Then wrap the other fingers around the handle.

ONE-HAND TRIGGERLIKE HOLD

26 ACROSS THE PALM

In order to form the perfect grip, whatever version you use, the handle must run diagonally across the palm of your left hand so that it rests from the point where the fingers and pad meet, across the palm to the middle of the forefinger. The handle should not sit all in the palm nor rest totally in the base of the fingers, but somewhere between those two positions. Try this simple correct grip test below.

HANDLE TOO HIGH
If you place the handle too high across the palm of your left hand, you will misdirect the angle of attack.

HANDLE TOO LOW
Grip too low across the base of the fingers and the angle of club shaft to club face to ball will be misaligned.

PERFECT POSITION
The handle extends slightly beyond the palm and runs down the top of the pad to the middle of the forefinger.

27 WEAK GRIP – OPEN FACE

The hands control the club face, and where you place your hands on the handle determines the alignment of your body at address. A weak grip with only one knuckle visible forces your body to aim left for a "fade" *(see p.52)*.

US Masters and Open Champion Nick Faldo prefers this one-knuckle grip

CURVE TO THE RIGHT

One knuckle showing indicates your body aims left while your club face is on target. The ball will fade or bend left-to-right

V formed by thumb and forefinger points to left of chin

28 STRONG GRIP – CLOSED FACE

A strong grip, with three knuckles showing, forces your body alignment to aim to the right while the club face faces the target directly. The ball will "draw," that is travel right-to-left in the air *(see p.53)*.

With this grip, the position of the body alignment is forced to aim right to curve the ball

CURVE TO THE LEFT

Club face alignment puts spin on the ball at impact to make it curve right-to-left. Practice with a longer club, such as a 4- or 5-iron, for best results

Three knuckles visible

29 GRIP FOR A PUTTER

The putting grip is more a question of personal choice. You need to eliminate any wrist action and to increase control of the club face. Almost all putters have a flat-fronted grip surface. This also dictates a slightly different grip, with the right thumb sitting more directly on top of the grip handle, facing down the putter handle and shaft.

1 Set the putter head on the ground and place the last three fingers of the left hand at right angles to the handle.

2 Bring across the right hand and place the first three fingers of that hand underneath at right angles to the handle.

3 Place the left thumb down the center of the handle, right-hand thumb at the ready. Keep all the fingers close together.

4 Now bring over the right thumb and place it on top of the left thumb. Keep the thumbs pointing down the shaft.

5 The forefinger of the left hand overlaps the fingers of the right hand, while the little finger of the right hand also overlaps the left hand.

LIGHT BUT SECURE ▷
Maintain a light but secure grip. Allow the left forefinger and right little finger to overlap with the opposite hand.

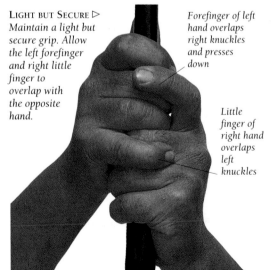

Forefinger of left hand overlaps right knuckles and presses down

Little finger of right hand overlaps left knuckles

30 THE LANGER GRIP

If you suffer from the "yips" – a total failure to sink short putts brought on by an attack of nerves that leads to a twitchy, stabbing action – learn from the pros. They suffer too. Bernhard Langer has tried many clubs (he once even adapted a secondhand ladies' putter) and several grip changes (*see below for his current successful one*).

1 With the left hand, grip the putter handle where it tapers into the shaft, and keep the arm straight.

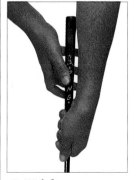

2 With fingers open, prepare to clasp both the putter handle and the forearm together.

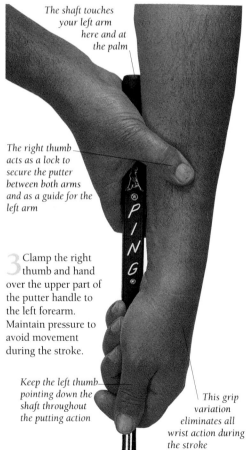

The shaft touches your left arm here and at the palm

The right thumb acts as a lock to secure the putter between both arms and as a guide for the left arm

3 Clamp the right thumb and hand over the upper part of the putter handle to the left forearm. Maintain pressure to avoid movement during the stroke.

Keep the left thumb pointing down the shaft throughout the putting action

This grip variation eliminates all wrist action during the stroke

ADDRESSING THE BALL

31 TAKING GOOD AIM

Most golf errors occur before the swing begins – when you set up and address the ball. To aim your body correctly, your feet, knees, hips, and shoulders must be on a line parallel to the ball-to-target line. Only then can you swing effectively and deliver the club face squarely to the back of the ball. Picture a railroad line first (*see right*), then place a club on the ground to set the "track" on target. Use this to set up.

◁ **DOWN THE LINE**
Visualize standing on one rail of a track with the ball resting on the other.

Your body is not aligned to the target but parallel with the ball-to-target line

Line the bottom edge of the club face square to the target

Let both shoulders hang down limply to eliminate tension, with elbows pointing to hips

Keep the left arm straight with the right arm slightly bent and relaxed. Maintain the hands over the ball

THREE BALL POSITIONS

32 THREE IDEAL BALL POSITIONS

There are three ideal ball positions around which you should build your stance, as shown (*see left*):
- A driver, the longest club, rests just inside the left instep or heel to look at the target.
- A medium No.5- or 6-iron will look at the target when you place it midway between the center of your stance and your left heel.
- A short, highly lofted club puts the ball in the center of your stance.

33 FOLLOWING A SIMPLE SETUP ROUTINE

There are three stages to a simple setup, as shown below:
- Orient toward your target.
- Align the club face to the target.
- Align your body to the club.

These steps will help you to achieve the best body posture and club face alignment every time. Begin by gripping the club (*see pp.22–27*) with your arms out in front.

Think where to send the ball, not how to swing

View the target, check hazards, and gauge the distance needed

Watch the ball and keep the chin up for the body rotation

1 Keep both hands on the grip and consider the options presented to you by the length, lie, and terrain of the hole.

2 Position your body around the club and ball. Align the club face so that its bottom edge is facing square to the target.

3 Align your body at right angles to the bottom edge of the club. Be sure your body is now parallel to the target line.

34 PERFECT POSTURE

When considering your posture, think about "stick people" with straight lines, angles, and no curves. First stand erect to the ball; then lean over from the hips, not from the waist. Your spine should still be relatively straight so that it can rotate easily. Feel the hips and pelvis area sit back out of the way so that the "belt line" of your trousers, shorts, or skirt is at an angle to the ground rather than parallel with it.

Keep the back straight and bend over from the hips

The arms hang down freely

Shoulder to arm to knee in a fairly perpendicular line

Bend the knees and keep them springy

CLASSIC POSTURE FOR ADDRESSING THE BALL

35 SETTING THE HEAD

Keep the chin up in every sense, and do not let it settle down onto the chest. Imagine that you are looking "down your nose" at the ball. This will set your head, and the shoulders will be free to to turn fully and easily in the backswing.

INCORRECT POSTURE △
If you let the chin lead the head down to the chest, this will cause a very steep angle of attack and restrict the swing.

CORRECT POSTURE △
Keeping the chin out from the chest will enable your shoulders and upper body to turn easily for a free-flowing swing.

36 SETTING THE SHOULDERS

Loosen up to avoid any tension in the shoulders and neck. Let both shoulders hang down limply at address. To line up a short- or medium-length iron, imagine a straight line running from your left shoulder to left arm, down the shaft.

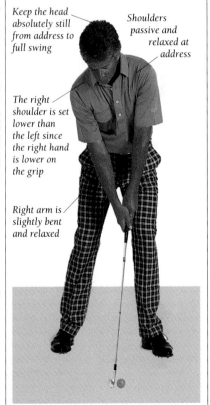

Keep the head absolutely still from address to full swing

Shoulders passive and relaxed at address

The right shoulder is set lower than the left since the right hand is lower on the grip

Right arm is slightly bent and relaxed

POSTURE HANGS FROM THE SHOULDERS

37 KEEPING THE SPINE STRAIGHT

Only by leaning over from the hips can the lower spine be comfortably straight. This is vital for swinging the club on the correct swing plane.

38 TESTING YOUR POSTURE

When standing over the ball, if you suspend a club from the center of the right shoulder, and it brushes your right knee, then you know you have perfect posture.

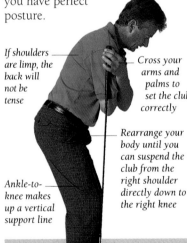

If shoulders are limp, the back will not be tense

Cross your arms and palms to set the club correctly

Rearrange your body until you can suspend the club from the right shoulder directly down to the right knee

Ankle-to-knee makes up a vertical support line

PROPER POSTURE TEST

39 AIMING BEYOND THE BALL

Keep your chin up and look down at the back, not the top of the ball. Then find a secondary marker, such as a divot mark, just in front of the ball, and on your intended target line. Aim the club face directly over that. This is easier and more accurate than aiming at a more distant target.

40 "CLOCKING ON"

Imagine that your feet are standing on, or parallel to, the two hands of a circular clock. Stand with both feet facing outward, the left foot parallel to 11 o'clock, the right foot at approximately 1 o'clock. Alternatively, place the right foot at a right angle to the ball-to-target line, and place the left foot pointing slightly to the left. Choose the stance that gives you perfect balance.

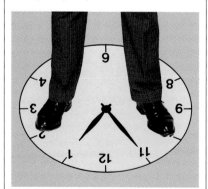

FEET AT "FIVE-TO-ONE" FOR FULL SWING

41 WEIGHT DISTRIBUTION

Remember these simple weight percentages for optimum balance: for long irons and woods lean 60:40 to your right side; 50:50 for mid-irons; shift your weight 60 percent to the left foot for lofted, short clubs.

60:40 RATIO FOR WOODS AND LONG IRONS

50:50 RATIO FOR MIDRANGE IRONS

40:60 RATIO FOR SHORT IRONS AND WEDGES

SWING WITH SUCCESS

42 THE SWING PLANE

Achieving the right swing plane is a vital part of ball control. Imagine that a length of crepe paper, or a streamer, is attached to the club face. As you take away and follow through past the ball, this paper will create a visible arc. This swing arc has a plane which is predetermined by the design of the club you use. A wood or long iron, for instance, dictates a shallow swing plane. If you had a club extended to 50 ft (15 m), this would demand a highly horizontal swing plane.

◁ **STEEP SWING PLANE**
Shorter, more lofted clubs determine a steeper take-away swing and a shallower forward swing.

Chin up and inclined a little to the right

The upper body turns, tilting only a little, as the arms swing upward in the backswing

Visualize a streamer on the club

◁ **SHALLOW SWING PLANE**
A long club, like a driver, determines a shallower swing plane. The forward swing is also flatter than the backswing.

43 Relaxed & Ready

Before you swing, you should feel in a state of relaxed readiness. Every part of your body above the line of the shaft – the hands, arms, back, and shoulders – should feel passive and relaxed. Every part below that line – feet, knees, and legs – should feel springy.

44 Spring Loading

Like a spring coiling, the upper body turns easily and the lower body responds. Feel your weight transfer onto your right foot, but not beyond it. The posture of the spine remains unchanged.

◁ Ideal Address
Bend the knees slightly and bend over gently from the hips.

Keep the chin up

Stand erect to the ball with hips, knees, and feet all giving support

Arms hang down freely, not rigidly straight

◁ Top of the Swing
At the top of the backswing, your back should be facing the target. Your shoulders have turned a full 90°.

The upper body rotates more than the hips

Weight shifts from left to right side

Left knee folds to the right

45 TOP OF BACKSWING

Here is a good way to judge if you have the club face in its ideal "hitting position" at the top of the backswing.

- Feel the left thumb sit under the handle as if "hitching a ride."
- The wrists are hinged now that the upper body has coiled fully .

MAINTAIN A LIGHT HOLD ON THE HANDLE

46 FORWARD SWING

The arms and hands swing the club down easily in a "free fall." The power and club head speed comes from:

- The rotation of your hips and torso toward the target.
- The transfer of weight to the left side.

Avoid rushing the club head to the ball. Instead, let it be swung freely through it.

Keep your head behind the ball at impact

Maintain the hinge of the wrists for extra power

Feel the club head lag behind

Right knee stays bent

HOW TO PROMOTE LAG
The right elbow should fall down to the right hip at the same time as the weight transfers to the left foot. This is the perfect way to begin the forward swing. It promotes the essential lag of the club head and prevents you from attempting to hit the ball too early.

A SWISH – NOT A HIT ▷
Do not think about "hitting" the ball. Instead, imagine "swishing" the club head through the ball.

47 A BALANCED FINISH

Keep your chin inclined to the right until your hands have swished the club head through the ball. The whole body turns toward the target and the weight transfers fully to the left side. Allow the head to respond to the turn of your body, and finally come up to look at the target in a perfectly balanced finish.

The head is pulled up by the rotation of the body after impact

The left shoulder moves backward

The right shoulder comes around and under the chin

BALANCED FEET ▽
Let the right heel come off the ground for a full, free turn to the target.

48 WHICH WEDGE?

To achieve height plus control, use the generous loft supplied by the wedge. The thick shoulder on the sole of a sand wedge glides the club smoothly through sand. The leading edge of a pitching wedge sits flush with the ground for easier loft from bare lies. Utility wedges serve either.

PITCHING WEDGE **UTILITY WEDGE**

49 PITCH & SPIN

A pitching wedge induces a much steeper angle of attack. For best control, crispness of shot, and backspin, aim to take ball-then-grass. Never attempt to scoop the club head under the ball. Also, a 3-piece ball responds better to spin (*see p.18*).

STEEP ATTACK INDUCES BACKSPIN

50 PITCHING A TEE

To get the correct feel of a pitch, put a tee a few inches beyond your ball in line with the target. Forget the ball and swing through to the tee, letting the club face glide down and through the ball, and on, to take the tee toward the target. Imagine the club face "passing through" the ball.

AIM FOR THE TEE

51 BRUSHING GRASS

When chipping, never scoop the club head under the ball. To take the ball up, swing the club down to take the ball first, then the grass. Aim to brush the grass just after the ball and always keep your hands in front of the club head.

Head stays still on contact

◁ BALL IN THE WAY
The ball lies in the way of the swing: let the club "pass" through the ball. Its loft makes the ball rise and roll.

52 WRISTBAND DRILL

Practice this drill to help you overcome the temptation to flick the club head under the ball with the left hand when chipping or putting. Hook the butt of a club handle inside a sweatband on your left wrist. Keep chipping until you achieve the correct feel of the arms and hands, leading the club head with a firm, rather than "melting," wrist.

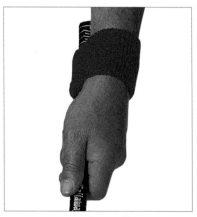

AVOID THE "WRISTY" FLICK

53 PERFECTING YOUR BUNKER ESCAPE

Don't be afraid of the sand shots. Aim to make a full swing, keeping the hands ahead as the club head enters the sand about 1 in (2–3 cm) behind the ball. Never attempt to scoop the ball out. Rather, glide the club face on a long, shallow arc through the sand below the ball taking sand-and-ball out.

Focus a few inches (centimeters) behind the ball

Shoulder to arm to hand to club shaft forms a straight line

Shoulders to arms to grip form a triangle

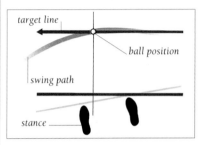

target line

ball position

swing path

stance

△ CHANGE OF ADDRESS
Align your shoulders, hips and feet 3–6 ft (1–2 m) to the left of the target.

WHERE TO STAND IN THE SAND ▷
Align yourself to the left of the target, but aim the club face directly toward the target.

WRIGGLE YOUR FEET WELL INTO THE SAND

54 SECURING A FIRM BASE IN SAND

If the sand is light and powdery, twist your feet well into it to secure a good platform for your swing. Your body weight should lean to the left to promote a "downward and through" swing as the club face glides through the sand. In coarse, wet sand you'll need a more powerful swing.

55 BURIED IN SAND

If your ball is plugged in the sand, set yourself up with the club face and body aligned square to the target, but with the ball well back in the stance. With your weight firmly on the left foot, swing the club up steeply, hinging the wrists early in the takeaway. Aim to bury the club in the sand just behind the ball. The force of impact "blasts" the ball out.

THE BALL GOES OUT ON A CUSHION OF SAND

56 GLIDING A TEE

To overcome those fears of bunker shots, try this visualization technique. Imagine that there is a tee hidden in the sand where your ball is sitting. Now forget the ball and swing as if you are hitting the tee onto the green right up there by the hole. The key is to let the club face glide through the sand.

Keep your head still while your eyes observe the sand-with-ball hit

The left shoulder moves back and up

The left knee has come around the ball

Bend the right knee at impact

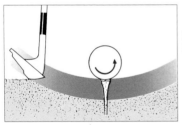

△ HIDDEN TEE
Visualize a tee hidden in the sand about 1 in (3 cm) deep. Aim to take the tee, not the ball.

HIT THE TEE ▷
Practice swinging through the "hidden" tee and the sand.

57 DON'T USE FORCE IN THE BUNKER

Because bunker shots seem so tricky, it is very tempting to rush the club down too quickly in order to hit that trapped ball out of the sand.

But you don't have to use applied force. Just feel the body rotate, the weight transfer to the left foot, and the club lag behind the hands.

Don't move your head until the right shoulder comes under the chin

Right shoulder moves under the chin

The hips rotate to the left, creating the space for the arms and legs

The right knee moves over from the right, enabling the weight to shift onto the left side as the hips rotate

GETTING THE RIGHT DISTANCE
Practice with 10–20 balls, varying the amount of sand you take with each ball, while still keeping the same amount of swing. This is a useful way to get used to sandshot distance and an alternative to varying your swing style. The less sand you scoop, the greater the distance you cover.

◁ **LAGGING BEHIND**
The club head should not overtake the hands until after you have splashed the sand and taken the ball.

Club face lags behind and still faces target

58 KEEPING HIPS STILL

When putting, let your arms hang comfortably, but point your elbows more inward, toward each hip, rather than outward. If the hips stay still, so will the knees and legs.

THE HIPS CREATE A STEADY BASE

59 ARCHING THE WRISTS

Arch the wrists as if forcing the putter head downward. This will help to "set" them securely, keeping them inactive, as if in splints or casts.

WRISTS ARCHED TO KEEP THEM PASSIVE

60 HINGING FROM THE HIPS

For the correct putting posture, stand erect and lean over from the hips. Keep your hips comfortably still. Practice this posture often in front of a mirror to see the correct address and to achieve the feel of creating a steady base for putting.

PUTTING POSTURE
Correct posture is vital. Lean over from the hips with a straight lower back.

Left shoulder sits a little higher than the right, parallel to the target line

Forefinger overlaps fingers of the right hand

61 HOW TO PUTT DOWNHILL

Downhill putts on fast greens often scare players and lead to tentative shots for fear the ball will race away. The best way to tackle this is to play the ball off the toe or heel of the putter. Stand back and assess the slope's severity. Pick a target in front of the hole for the ball to reach before the slope's contour takes over. Strike the toe or heel away from the sweet spot so the ball leaves the putter "dead."

◁ TOE HIT
Strike the toe of the club to keep the ball from racing away.

Toe

◁ HEEL HIT
Hit the heel of the club, not the sweet spot in the center.

Heel

62 PREPARING TO PUTT

Achieve the smoothness of movement that is vital for a successful putt by avoiding tension. Let the shoulders, arms, and hands hang down comfortably. Keep the elbows pointing slightly more inward, toward each hip, rather than outward. Hold the lower back straight after leaning over from the hips, with the wrists arched as though forcing the putter head downward.

Keep shoulders relaxed and the head will stay still

Body weight is slightly left of center

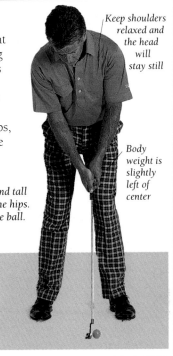

STAND UPRIGHT ▷
Do not hunch up: stand tall and lean over from the hips. Look directly over the ball.

◁ CLUB HEAD TO BALL POSITION
Try suspending the putter head just above the ground. Some players prefer this for a steadier address.

63 THE PUTT SWING PATH

A useful tip to remember when putting is that the putter should track away in a very slight arc – it should not swing in a straight line away from the target. On the forward swing, though, the putter does travel in a straight line through to the target.

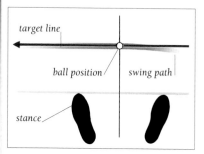

target line

ball position / swing path

stance

Observe the putter face as it moves away

Left wrist is straight throughout the stroke

Maintain a slight kink in your right wrist

△ SLIGHT ARC
The backswing of your putt should arc slightly away from the target, and not go straight back.

SWING THOUGHT ▷
Think of the ball as lying in the way of your swing, rather than concentrating on how to hit it.

A MUG IS AN IDEAL INDOOR TARGET

64 DEALING WITH PUTTING DISTANCE

Judging distances for putts presents a challenge, especially since you may have a long 100-ft (30-m) putt, followed by a short shot of only 3 ft (1 m). Try this drill at home: spend 10 minutes putting with your eyes closed into a mug on the carpet. After each putt, and before opening your eyes, try to gauge by "feel" whether the ball was short or long, and if it rested to the left or right of the mug.

65 SEEING THE BUTT

To get the correct depth of grip for a putt, set the putter head on the ground and sit the right thumb pad over the left thumb on the grip (*see p.28*). Make sure that you have at least ½ in (1 cm) of the end (the butt) of the putter handle visible.

THE RIGHT AMOUNT OF BUTT

66 FINDING A PRIMARY TARGET

Most putting greens are not flat but have a slope or contour that will make the ball break to the left or right. First assess the slope's severity and then pick a primary target – a point on the green where the ball's roll will be affected by that slope. You must still aim to putt straight, but straight to that primary target.

67 PACING IT RIGHT

More second putts are missed because the first one was struck too softly or firmly, not because the putt was too wide of the hole. Pace is more critical than direction. Here's the best way to judge pace and distance: practice putting from 30 yds (30 m) and set yourself a target area wider than the hole – say, 3 ft (1 m) wide – to aim for.

68 THINKING TRIANGLES

Concentrate on the total stroke, which is one third backward swing and two thirds forward swing. Think "one third back, two thirds through" to help you maintain control of the complete putt, even for short shots. Imagine a triangle that hangs down from your shoulders, through your chest, and tapers down your arms to point at your grip. Notice that, while the shoulders have a smooth, rocking pendulumlike action, the triangle always stays intact. Arms, hands, and putter just come along for a ride!

THE ARC OF THE PUTT
The geometry of the putt goes like this: the shoulders, arms, and putter go back on a slight arc inside the target line. On short putts this arc is hardly noticeable. Keeping the club head close to the ground in the backswing creates the arc naturally. You must have the club face looking at the target on the forward swing.

GETTING THE FEEL RIGHT
First roll a ball underhand to your circular target. Feel how much back swing it took to roll it that far. Now practice putting with the same feel.

Allow yourself a generous target area, say 1 yd (1 m) in circumference for long-distance putts. The object is to pace it, not to hole it

Left shoulder marginally higher than right

Left shoulder comes down a little

Line across shoulders stays parallel to target line

CONTROL ON THE COURSE

69 MAINTAINING YOUR BALANCE UPHILL

Golf courses are sprinkled with hazards and contoured with awkward lies. They are there to challenge your game – to make you think. For uphill shots, align your shoulders parallel to the slope and let your weight settle on the lower foot. Position the ball nearer the higher foot and aim a little to the right to compensate for the ball's natural tendency to fly to the left.

◁ THREE KEYS TO RECOVERY
Aim to swing the club through the ball, make good contact, and feel balanced during the swing, and after it!

Feel the swing coming from the arms on a slope, as it's hard to do two full body turns

△ CLUB CHOICE
A rising slope gives the club face an increased loft at address. So take a less lofted club for the same trajectory.

△ SELECT A LOWER LOFT
A 6-iron effectively does the work of an 8-iron on an elevated slope, so you need to select the less-lofted club.

70 UPHILL RECOVERY

On an uphill slope you are more than likely to lose your balance in the backswing, so do not attempt a full backswing. Allow the club to travel in a naturally flat or shallow swing plane rather than taking it up with your arms. Aim to sweep the ball up the slope.

LOSS OF BALANCE ▷
Avoid trying to complete a full backswing uphill.

71 DOWNHILL PLAY

For a downhill shot, your balance will naturally veer forward, with the head almost over the lower foot. The backswing will involve the arms lifting the club up steeply while the lower body struggles to stay in balance. Swing down the slope. Avoid a wrist action that picks the ball up off the surface.

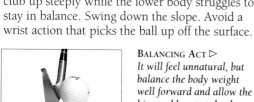

△ **MORE LOFT NEEDED**
Use a more lofted, less powerful, club and aim to the left to achieve the same result as on even ground.

BALANCING ACT ▷
It will feel unnatural, but balance the body weight well forward and allow the hips and legs to take the strain to stay balanced.

Position yourself with the ball near the higher foot, which is the back foot this time

△ **LAND IT SHORT**
Play to land the ball short of the green as the ball flies lower and rolls farther on downhill shots.

72 BALL ABOVE STANCE

Stand a little taller than usual when playing across a slope. The ball is above the level of your feet, which means that you are standing closer to it. To adjust your stance you need to shorten your grip and lean into the slope with your body weight more toward the toes than on the heels. The ball should be played in the center of your stance for longer clubs, and there is no need to aim right.

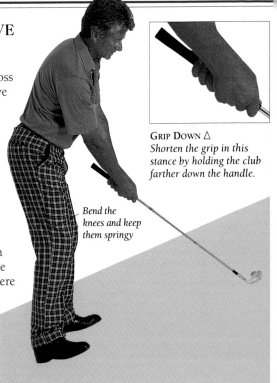

GRIP DOWN △
Shorten the grip in this stance by holding the club farther down the handle.

Bend the knees and keep them springy

LOFTED CLUB ADDRESS ▷
If you are playing a shorter, more lofted club, bring the ball even nearer the right foot, and play it back in the stance.

BALL NEARER YOUR RIGHT FOOT IN STANCE

73 RIGHT OF CENTER

For steeper slopes, play the ball slightly nearer your right foot to allow for the ball bending to the left. The adjusted stance for playing across a slope will make the angle or arc you create when swinging away from, and into, the ball flatter than normal. This will in turn cause the ball to "hook"; that is, to move in a curve from right to left in the air.

74 BALL BELOW STANCE

To play this uncomfortable but not uncommon shot, bend the knees more and keep the weight on the heels. Lengthen the grip. With the ball in the center of the stance, the steepness of the swing plane will cause the ball to veer to the right, so aim a little to the left. You need very little body movement in this stroke. It is an "arms mainly" swing.

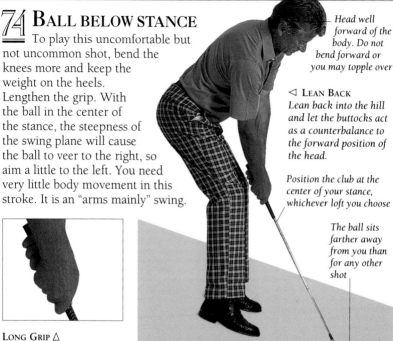

Head well forward of the body. Do not bend forward or you may topple over

◁ **LEAN BACK**
Lean back into the hill and let the buttocks act as a counterbalance to the forward position of the head.

Position the club at the center of your stance, whichever loft you choose

The ball sits farther away from you than for any other shot

LONG GRIP △
Lengthen the grip and bring the butt of the handle onto the palm of your left hand.

75 RESTRICTED SWING

Standing above the ball with it lying below the level of your stance forces you to make a very steep angle of attack. Such a steep swing plane means that you can hardly present the club face square to the target at impact. Instead, your club will face to the right at impact, which sends the ball farther to the right. So aim to the left to make the natural left-to-right flight generally more on target.

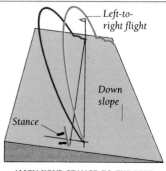

Left-to-right flight

Down slope

Stance

ALIGN YOUR STANCE TO THE LEFT

76 FADING THE BALL

Shaping your shots is not as hard as it sounds, and once mastered can get you around tricky obstacles like trees. To "fade" a ball so that it sets off to the left and bends in the air back to the right (and on to the target), align the club face to the target by adopting a weak grip (see p.27) in which your hands rotate a little to the left on the handle. Your body alignment will be "open" (to the left).

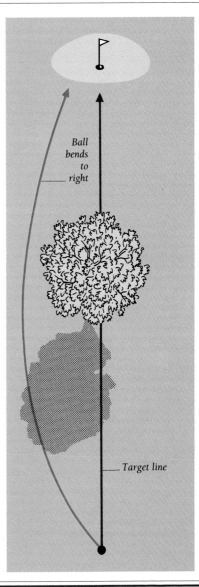

Ball
bends
to
right

Target line

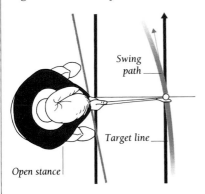

Swing
path

Target line

Open stance

△ OPEN CLUB FACE
The open club face sets the ball off to the left. It bends right as it slows down in the air.

△ OPEN STANCE
The alignment of shoulders, hips, knees, and feet are forced into an "open" position; that is, they are aimed to the left.

BENDING RIGHT ▷
Swing the club along the line of your stance and then watch the ball fade.

77 DRAWING THE BALL

To draw the ball so that it sets off to the right but bends to the left in the air back on to the target, align the club face to target and adopt a strong grip (*see p.27*). Your body alignment is forced into a "closed" (to the right) position and is aimed to the right. Because of your closed alignment you will be on a shallower swing plane, which in turn causes the ball to fly lower and roll farther.

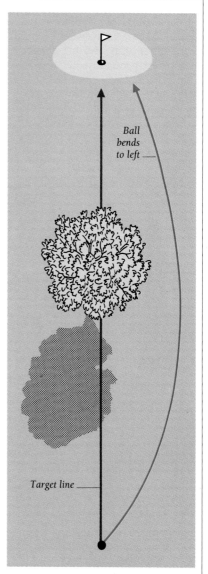

Ball bends to left

Target line

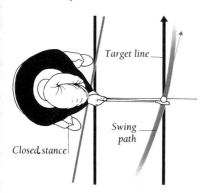

Target line

Swing path

Closed stance

△ CLOSED FACE
The closed club face sets the ball off to the right. It bends to the left as it slows down in the air.

△ CLOSED STANCE
The club faces the target but a strong grip guarantees that the club will travel across the target line on an inside-out path.

BENDING LEFT ▷
Swing the club along the line of your stance and then watch the ball draw.

78 VARYING THE TEE

For irons, make sure that only the cup is visible with the ball just touching the top of the grass. The club head will meet the ball on a slightly descending path. For woods, you are sweeping the ball away. The tee should sit up so that you can achieve an easy, sweeping action through impact.

HIGHER TEE FOR LESS LOFTED CLUB

4-WOOD ▷
Use a lower tee for such lofted woods.

◁ 3-WOOD
Use a low tee for shallow-faced woods.

79 DRIVING IN WINDY CONDITIONS

Varying the tee is a neglected but vital part of the strategic game. For woods, you should be able to see half the ball above the top of the wood. Deep-faced woods need even higher tees. But wind affects this half-ball rule. In windy conditions, it is best to tee off into the wind with a slightly higher tee; this actually promotes a flatter swing plane and lower ball flight. When driving downwind, use a lofted wood and lower tee.

80 IN THE ROUGH

Long, rough grass is a common hazard when you veer off the fairway. If your ball sits deep in the rough, hold a lofted club, such as a 9-iron or wedge, firmly, and play the shot powerfully with the ball closer to the back foot. Use an early wrist break and take a steep upward and downward swing of the arms. Keep the right knee bent and the eyes down. Your priority is to get back on the fairway.

USE A NO.9 IRON OR WEDGE

STRENGTHS & WEAKNESSES

81 STRENGTHENING YOUR WRISTS

Strong wrists guarantee more efficient play – ideally your left and right wrists should be of equal strength. Here is an easy exercise for improving your grip without straining your wrists. Flexing a soft ball, as shown below, will help you strengthen your wrist muscles. Make this part of a preround warmup session.

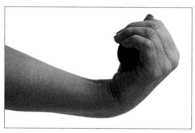

PALM PRESSURE △
Cupping the wrists adds extra muscle tension in the palm pressure drill. Start with a 20- to 30-second routine with each hand.

WRIST BUILDUP △
Hold a soft ball, palm upward. Squeeze the ball and relax. Repeat until you feel the pressure in your forearm. Swap hands.

82 VISUALIZE SUCCESS

Always try to picture what you want to achieve with each shot. For instance, visualize the ball landing on the green before you chip on to it. Remember the saying, "When the mind can perceive it, the body can achieve it."

83 ACT LIKE A PRO

Observe how pros behave at a tournament. They are always neatly dressed; they care for their equipment; they don't take reckless risks; they show respect for other players and the golf course; and they don't complain about losing.

84 MEMORIZE THE SWING'S IMAGE

Your swing is a sequence of muscle movements. You can memorize these effectively and re-create them with a simple series of swings without the club. Before you play, practice the full golf swing and recognize the feel of the correct swing movements in front of a full-length mirror. Watch the reactions of the body and mark on the mirror where your head is reflected. Swing without moving off the mark.

Palms face outward and flat

Weight transfers to left side, hips rotate, and right heel lifts

Keep looking down at where the ball would be

Place hands flat and back-to-back

Assume your normal teeing off position

Lean over the hips in the take-away and rotate the upper body to the right

1 Take up your standard stance, with hands flat and facing back-to-back. Try to picture an effortless interaction of body moves.

2 As you lean over from the hips, rotate your upper body to the right, letting the hips, legs, and feet respond.

3 As you turn through the full swing, feel the weight transfer to the left side and the right heel lift completely off the ground.

85 CHANGE-HANDS DRILL

Take a medium iron and swing the club, again in front of a mirror, first with the right arm, then with the left. This exercise will familiarize you with the "feel" of the swing. Doing this with each arm individually helps build good muscle memory as well as good club control. Sense the movement coming from the rotation of the body rather than from a pickup of the arm. The body rotates as the arms swing up.

Place non-playing arm behind back

NATURAL SWING EXERCISE

86 UPSIDE-DOWN UMBRELLA

An open umbrella makes an ideal target for practice play. Use plastic balls and chip them into an opened umbrella positioned upside down and as far away as possible. Lob a few balls underhand into the umbrella, then apply the same feel when using the club. Later, try a set of 20 balls with your eyes closed. Trust your balance and rhythm.

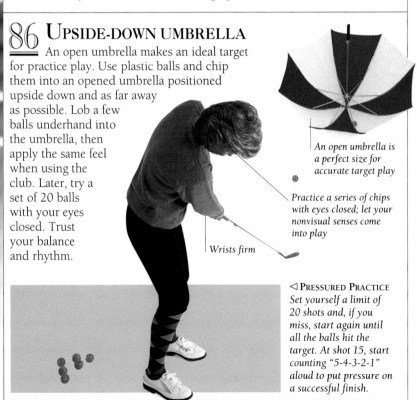

An open umbrella is a perfect size for accurate target play

Practice a series of chips with eyes closed; let your nonvisual senses come into play

Wrists firm

◁ **PRESSURED PRACTICE**
Set yourself a limit of 20 shots and, if you miss, start again until all the balls hit the target. At shot 15, start counting "5-4-3-2-1" aloud to put pressure on a successful finish.

87 TIRE TESTING

Practice your swing and strengthen your wrist with the aid of a car tire. Place it on the ground and swing into the tire one-handed (*as shown below*). Also try holding the club head and swinging the grip around the inside of the tire.

Relax your shoulders

◁ **FEEL THE FORCE**
As the arms swing the club freely downward, you will feel the weight transfer naturally as the club head accelerates into the tire.

WRIST MUSCLES ▷
Hold a club one-handed by the club head inside the tire. Move your wrists so that the club hits both sides of the rim.

Right arm behind back

The body rotates as the arm swings down

Feel the club head lag behind, then hit the tire

Begin slowly at first, then speed up the hits

88 SWINGING WITH NO ARMS

Try upper body stretches and swings without the club to help strengthen your swing action and develop "muscle memory"; that is, knowing by instinct that you are naturally using the correct movements of the swing. Before you play a round of golf, practice the full golf swing "with no arms" as shown below. Also repeat this at home in front of a mirror and observe how your body moves.

Focus on where the ball would be

Arms in "cross-your-heart" position

Turn your head to follow the body and imaginary ball direction

Turn the shoulders and upper body, letting the left shoulder come under the chin as the right one goes backward

Rotate the hips to give your swing plenty of balance

Hip rotation causes the right knee to come around

1 Assume the address position except for the arms, which should be crossed over the chest.

2 Swing back and feel the upper body turn easily. Feel the lower body respond.

3 As your body swings forward, feel how the movement is reversed and the upper body responds.

89 SHOULDER & WAIST WARMUP

This is a useful swing-related exercise that simulates the actual motion of the golf swing. It sets your upper body – the engine room of your swing – into the correct backward and forward motion. Practice this for 20 complete swings before hitting any balls.

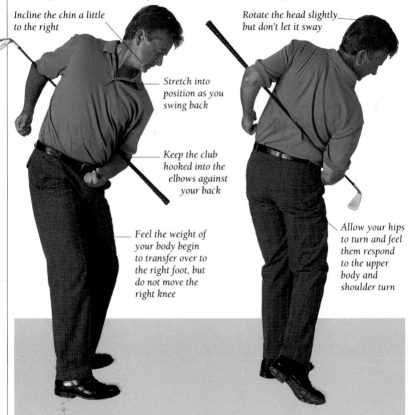

Incline the chin a little to the right

Stretch into position as you swing back

Keep the club hooked into the elbows against your back

Feel the weight of your body begin to transfer over to the right foot, but do not move the right knee

Rotate the head slightly but don't let it sway

Allow your hips to turn and feel them respond to the upper body and shoulder turn

1 Hook the club across your back so that it rests horizontally in the crook of both elbows. Rotate your shoulders through 90° for a backswing.

2 Rotate your body as you would on the downswing and then an additional 90° to the followthrough position. Feel the muscles loosening up.

90 LOOSENING THE BACK

You must loosen the muscles in your lower back and stretch your spine before hitting your first ball of the day. This will help you to avoid instant swing stiffness as well as long-term back trouble, the most common golf-related injury. Perform this back-loosening warmup exercise 20 times until you feel the benefits.

Stretch both arms fully above your head, gripping the club horizontally. Repeat 10 times

Bring the club down slowly and gradually bend your back with head tucked down

Relax, and don't come up too quickly

STRETCH & BEND
Try this two-part lower back loosener with or without a more traditional warmup touching the toes. Keep the feet shoulder-width apart throughout.

SET YOUR OWN PRACTICE GREEN TARGETS

91 PRACTICE PUTTING GREEN

Over half your shots over 18 holes of a golf course will be putts, so never neglect this very demanding part of the game. It is easy to assume that your greatest priority in golf is to practice your swing on a driving range, but putting on a practice green is equally important. Do not simply hit balls, but rather set yourself a target, such as three putts for each hole and then two for the next round of putts.

92 KNOWING YOUR DISTANCE

Each wood and iron is designed to make the ball react differently, and to conform to a certain achievable loft and distance (*see tables below and opposite*). However, very few golfers can say for certain how far they hit each club in their bag. You may never hit the same consistent distances as the pros, but it is possible to calculate your average hitting distance for each club. Take 20 balls to a practice tee. Hit them with one club. Now walk over and pick up the five nearest and five farthest. The 10 grouped in the center will give you your average distance for that club. Mark it down on a scorecard or notebook. Now repeat this process using all the other clubs in your bag. This will help you when you are playing and you know you have to hit, say, 165 yds (150 m): you can instantly select the correct club.

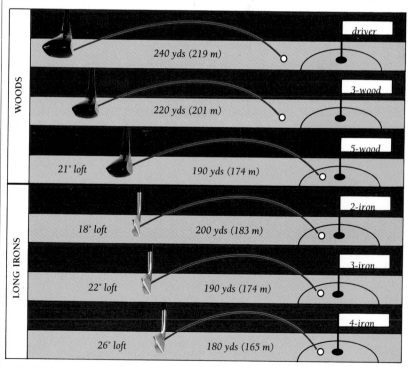

WOODS

driver — 240 yds (219 m)

3-wood — 220 yds (201 m)

5-wood — 21° loft — 190 yds (174 m)

LONG IRONS

2-iron — 18° loft — 200 yds (183 m)

3-iron — 22° loft — 190 yds (174 m)

4-iron — 26° loft — 180 yds (165 m)

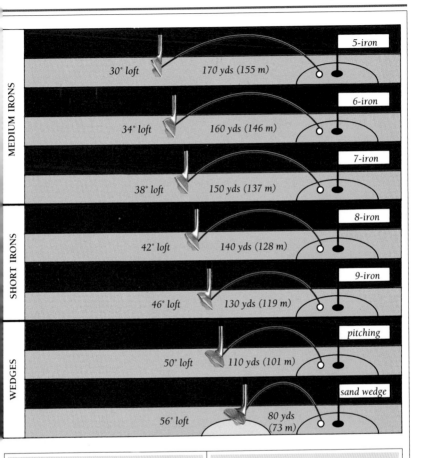

MEDIUM IRONS

5-iron — 30° loft — 170 yds (155 m)

6-iron — 34° loft — 160 yds (146 m)

7-iron — 38° loft — 150 yds (137 m)

SHORT IRONS

8-iron — 42° loft — 140 yds (128 m)

9-iron — 46° loft — 130 yds (119 m)

WEDGES

pitching — 50° loft — 110 yds (101 m)

sand wedge — 56° loft — 80 yds (73 m)

93 REMEMBER YOUR YARDAGE

The yardage of a hole is indicated by markers at the tee box and along the fairway. You must rely on this in conjunction with your scorecard and average hitting distance.

94 DRIVING RANGE

Be clear about what you are going to practice. Hitting a bucket of balls is not practice. Resolve to improve your swing path, then weight transfer, then rhythm, and so on. Achieve one goal at a time.

PLAYING THE GAME

95 KNOWING THE GOLF COURSE

Make a rough sketch of each hole of your local course in a notebook. Using one stride as roughly a yard, measure the distance to any hazards from the tee. Next, work out the distance to the front of the green from various points on the fairway. Finally, calculate the length of the green and the current pin position.

DRAW UP A GUIDE FOR EACH HOLE
Here is a par-4, 420-yd (370-m) hole showing you the typical key features and hazards to note down.

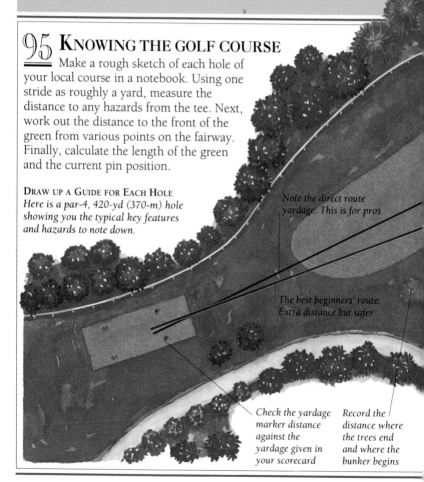

Note the direct route yardage. This is for pros

The best beginners' route. Extra distance but safer

Check the yardage marker distance against the yardage given in your scorecard

Record the distance where the trees end and where the bunker begins

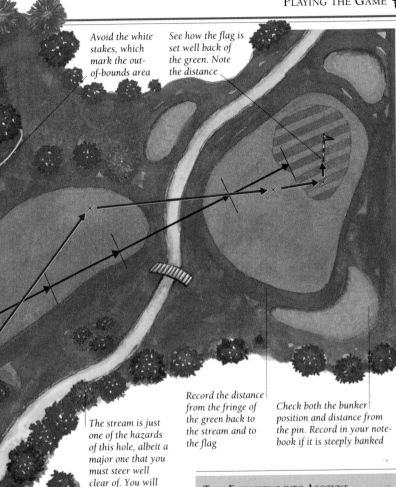

Avoid the white stakes, which mark the out-of-bounds area

See how the flag is set well back of the green. Note the distance

Record the distance from the fringe of the green back to the stream and to the flag

Check both the bunker position and distance from the pin. Record in your note-book if it is steeply banked

The stream is just one of the hazards of this hole, albeit a major one that you must steer well clear of. You will have to pitch or chip over it farther on

CHARTING THE HAZARDS
The trees and bunkers are the first hazards to note. You need to know how far they are to be able to land short of them, as well as the yardage to carry the ball over them. Note down the distances.

TAKE EVERYTHING INTO ACCOUNT
Bear in mind weather and ground conditions as well as the hazards and obstacles of the hole, plus the yardage needed. Add this to your knowledge of your average hitting distance (see p.62) and you can place your shots in the best position on the fairway. Think only one shot at a time.

96 UNDERSTANDING YOUR SCORECARD

Allow yourself time away from the course to study a scorecard and to understand what the entries mean. Failure to mark a card correctly, say, for your first 18-hole score or to acquire a handicap, can lead to disqualification. Golf rules are very strict on this point. Ask a playing partner or the local pro to explain the finer points of scoring.

Stableford is ideal for beginners

STABLEFORD OR MEDAL / STROKEPLAY
There are two basic scoring systems: Stableford is based on points-per-hole; medal play on shots-per-hole.

Par is the number of shots a pro is expected to take at each hole

Mark each other's score in the "A" column and your own in "Marker"

JULY 'STABLEFORD'

		DATE 21-5-95	H'CAP 24	STROKES RECEIVED 21

1st TEE — PLAYER A. K. RYAN — PLAYER B.

	SSS	PAR
BLUE	72	71
YELLOW	72	70
RED	74	74

Signed: M. Lunn

AUGUST MEDAL

		DATE 19-4-95	H'CAP 21

1st TEE — PLAYER A. J. HARRISON — PLAYER B.

	SSS	PAR
BLUE	72	71
YELLOW	72	70
RED	74	74

Signed: M. Lunn   James Harrison

First swap cards then mark your gross shot or points score in the "marker" column (first column)

"Player" and "Marker" check and agree on the score then sign each card at the end of a game

Let the ball drop at arm's length so that it won't hit your feet

DROPPING THE BALL △
Hold the ball at shoulder height, arm stretched, and release. Watch where the ball rests.

97 PLAYING BY THE RULES

The rules of golf cover the shape and size of golf clubs and ball, the scoring and handicap systems, and, on a local level, they warn you about out-of-bounds areas, special course hazards, and seasonal rules. Local rules appear on the back of the scorecard, so check them carefully. You must also observe golf etiquette – the common courtesies expected of any player, from inviting faster players through, to marking your scorecard in the next tee box.

MARKING YOUR BALL ▷
On the greens, mark your ball if it lies in your partner's line.

MARKERS △
Place a marker or coin behind the ball and remove the ball.

You may lift the ball for green repairs. Replace it on exactly the same spot

98 TENDING THE FLAG CORRECTLY

There are two basic rules to remember regarding flagsticks. If you are playing off the green toward the flagstick, it does not matter if your ball hits it. But once you are on the green it does matter. If you are putting from the green you must have the flagstick removed or attended. You should offer to attend the flag or remove it for your partner. Avoid creating any interfering shadows. Remove the flag as the ball draws near. If a putt is made on the green and the ball hits the flag, the player will incur a penalty.

FLAGSTICK ADVICE
Although not against the rules, it is good etiquette to prevent the end of the flagstick from touching the green as this might cause damage. You may stand behind, rather than to the side, of the hole when you have to avoid standing on the line of putt of another player.

Wait until the ball rests before placing the flag down

DON'T BE CASUAL △
Never throw down the flagstick. Lay it down on the ground with care.

Tend the flag clear of the hole and do not stand on another player's putting line

99 ESSENTIAL ETIQUETTE

There are 34 rules in the modern rule book as well as a vast number of sections and subsections dealing with specific details. (You should be entitled to one free copy of the rules if you are a club member.) But your chief concern should be golf etiquette – that is good on-course behavior and how it affects other players. This involves common sense and good manners but it must be mastered just like the game itself.

- Always replace your divots on the fairway and tread them in firmly.
- Rake the bunker after use with the rake provided.
- Repair your ball marks on the green immediately.
- Never take your cart or golfbag onto the tee box or onto putting greens.

Be ready to play your shot on the green

PUTTING PROCEDURE
The farthest away from the hole putts first. If that player putts, misses, and is still farthest away, he or she must putt next.

100 OBTAINING A HANDICAP

If you join a new club you must have, or establish, your handicap to play in competitions. Your average score over three games with a player who has a handicap, will be judged against the Standard Scratch Score. The SSS relates to the length of the course. If you average 100 shots and the SSS is 72, your handicap will be 28.

101 WORKING OUT YOUR SCORE

Once you have established your handicap, you deduct that figure from the gross or total number of strokes played to get your net or final score. A beginner with 28 is given an extra shot on each hole (18) plus 10 extra (18 + 10 = 28) strokes, designated to the most difficult holes as indicated by the stroke index on the scorecard.

INDEX

ACKNOWLEDGMENTS

Dorling Kindersley would like to thank Hilary Bird for compiling the index, Ann Kay for proofreading, Mark Bracey for computer assistance, and Richmond Golf Club for the loan of golf clubs and equipment.

Photography
All photographs by Matthew Ward and Stephen Bartholomew except for location photography by Philip Gatward.

Illustrations
Janos Marffy for line drawings.
Jane Pickering for color illustration 64–65.